IRISH SONGS FOR UKULELE

BY DICK SHERIDAN

ISBN 978-1-57424-283-6
SAN 683-8022

Cover by James Creative Group

Copyright © 2012 CENTERSTREAM Publishing, LLC
P.O. Box 17878 - Anaheim Hills, CA 92817

www.centerstream-usa.com

A DEDICATION
~To my sister Mary~
oOo
With a song in her heart,
especially if it's Irish.

Table Of Contents

About The Author...5

IRISH SONGS

A Little Bit Of Heaven.........................6

All For Me Grog 8

A Nation Once Again........................10

An Irish Lullaby...............................12

Arthur McBride 14

Band Played On, The.....................17

Believe Me If All Those
   Endearing Young Charms..........19

Black Velvet Band, The 22

Brennan On The Moor.....................25

Cockles And Mussels 27

Danny Boy 29

Dicey Riley 31

Do You Want Your Auld
   Lobby Washed Down...................33

Foggy Dew 36

Garryowen.......................................38

Harrigan 39

Hills Of Connemara, The 41

If You're Irish 42

I'll Take You Home
   Again, Kathleen..........................44

I'll Tell Me Ma 46

I Met Her In The Garden 48

Irish Rover, The 51

Irish Washerwoman 53

Kerry Dance, The 54

Little Beggarman, The....................56

Little Town in The
   Ould County Down.......................57

McNamara's Band 59

Mermaid, The 62

Merry Plowboy, The 64

Minstrel Boy, The.............................66

Miss McLeod's Reel........................68

Mother Machree..............................69

Mountains O' Mourne 71

Mrs. Murphy's Chowder 74

Mulligan Guard, The.......................77

My Irish Molly O...............................80

My Lagan Love 84

My Wild Irish Rose 87

Nellie Kelly......................................88

Paddy Works On The Railway 89

Peg O' My Heart..............................91

Rising Of The Moon 93

Rose Of Tralee, The 96

Sally Gardens.................................97

Spancil Hill 99

Star Of The County Down 101

Swallow Tail Jig.............................103

Sweet Rosie O'Grady 104

Waxies' Dargle, The.......................105

Wearing Of The Green 107

When Irish Eyes Are Smiling.........108

When You and I Were
   Young, Maggie...........................112

Where The River Shannon Flows...114

Whiskey In The Jar 116

Wild Rover, The..............................118

—~m~—

AN IRISH BLESSING

May the road rise up to meet you,

And may the wind be always at your back.

May the sun shine warm upon your face,

And the raindrops fall softly upon your field.

And until we meet again,

May God hold you in the small of His hand.

oOo

—~m~—

About The Author

Dick Sheridan began playing the ukulele in grade school, continued on through high school and college, and is still at it now many decades later. He comes by his love of Irish music naturally. Both his paternal great grandparents emigrated from the Emerald Isle, and if there is any truth to family legends and leprechauns, the Sheridans from County Cavan were definitely a musical clan.

Growing up in the 1940s, Dick was exposed to the wave of Irish-American music then being written and resurrected from the turn of the century. Radio, film, and recording stars like Bing Crosby, Dennis Day, and a host of "Irish" tenors did much to popularize these songs, and popular they were indeed! Everybody knew the songs and everybody sang them. Few households were without their phono- graphs or parlor pianos playing the Irish hit tunes of the day.

Dick's childhood enthusiasm for Ireland and Irish music further stemmed from living in the New York City area with its large population of Irish-American families and the annual celebration of St. Patrick's Day and the world renowned parade up Fifth Avenue. There was always the "wearin' of the green on March 17." Shamrocks were in all the windows and store fronts. Celluloid buttons proclaimed: "I'm Irish, Kiss Me!" Banners emblazoned with sayings like Erin Go Bragh hung on door fronts and lampposts, while Irish flags fluttered with their vibrant bands of green, white and orange.

Year after year the marching bands and bagpipe brigades played all the favorites until they became ingrained – "McCarthy pumped the old bassoon, Hennessey Tennessee tootled the flute" – and indeed the music was something grand.

Although the marchers down Fifth Avenue weren't likely to be playing ukuleles, there was plenty of opportunity elsewhere. All across America, wherever there was the lilt of Irish laughter, the strumming of ukuleles could be heard -- in homes, in dorm rooms and fraternity houses, in taverns, and in the festive meeting halls of the Friendly Sons of St. Patrick and the Ancient Order of Hibernians.

Celebrating revelers paid homage to him who drove the snakes from Ireland. But if there was a wee bit too much libation, the good saint's influenced failed on the morrow: Beware the Snakes Revenge.

In mature years Dick joined a musical group in the Syracuse, NY area called the Tipp Hill Gaels. Five in all, it included two native sons and a daughter from the auld sod, along with two Irish-Americans "proud of all the Irish that was in 'em!" It was during this time that he learned many of the authentic Irish songs and tunes included in this collection

Whether or not you boast a green carnation in your button-hole or an Irish tri-color in your bonnet, Dick hopes that whatever your heritage you'll enjoy the wealth of music contained in this book. There's always a welcome for an honorary Celt, lad or lass!

"May the saints preserve ye!"

THE WAXIES' DARGLE
"Says my old one to your old one ..."

A LITTLE BIT OF HEAVEN

Ukulele tuning: gCEA

J. KEIRN BRENNAN   **ERNEST R. BALL**

A LITTLE BIT OF HEAVEN

Besides "A Little Bit Of Heaven," composer Ernest Ball had other Irish-flavored
songs to his credit, including "Mother Machree" and "When Irish Eyes Are Smiling."
A chief collaborator was Chauncey Olcott whose Broadway production of THE HEART
OF PADDY WHACK introduced this song in 1914.

ALL FOR ME GROG

Ukulele tuning: gCEA

Traditional

Verse 1. Where is me hat, me nog-gin, nog-gin hat? All gone for gin and to - bac - co!___ And the

brim is wore out, and the crown is kicked a-bout, and me hair is look-ing out for bet-ter weath-er. Well, it's

Chorus: All for me grog, me jol-ly, jol-ly grog, all gone for beer and to - bac - co!___ For I

spent all me tin on the lass-ies drink-ing gin, now a - cross the west-ern o-cean I must wand - er

8

Verse 2.
Where is me hat, me nogin, nogin hat?
All gone for gin and tobacco!
And the brim is wore out,
And the crown is knocked about,
And me hair is looking out for better weather.
CHORUS

Verse 3.
Where is me shirt, me noggin, noggin shirt?
All gone for gin and tobacco!
And the sleeves are worn out,
And the collar's knocked about,
And the tails is looking out for better weather.
CHORUS

Verse 4.
Where are me boots, me noggin, noggin boots?
All gone for gin and tobacco!
And the soles are worn out,
And the heels are kicked about,
And me toes are looking out for better weather.
CHORUS

Verse 5.
Where are me pants, me noggin, noggin pants?
All gone for gin and tobacco!
And the cuffs are worn out,
And the fly is knocked about,
And me arse is looking out for better weather.
CHORUS

Verse 6.
I'm sick to me head, and I haven't been to bed,
Since I first came ashore with all me plunder;
I see centipedes and snakes,
And I'm full of pains and aches,
And I guess it's time to shove off over yonder.
CHORUS

A NATION ONCE AGAIN

Ukulele tuning: gCEA

Thomas Osborne Davis

A NATION ONCE AGAIN

Verse 2.

And from that time through wildest woe that hope has shown a far light,
Nor could love's brightest summer glow outshine that solemn starlight;
It seemed to watch above my head through forum field and fame,
It's angel voice sang round my bed, "A nation once again!"
CHORUS

Verse 3.

So, as I grow from boy to man, I bent to me that bidding,
My spirit of each selfish plan and cruel passion ridding;
For thus I hoped some day to aid, nor can such hope be vain,
When my dear country shall be made a nation once again.
CHORUS

AN IRISH LULLABY

Ukulele tuning: gCEA

JAMES ROYCE SHANNON

Verse 1. O - ver in Kil - lar - ney,_____ man - y years a - go, my

moth - er sang a song to me in tones so sweet and low; just a

sim - ple lit - tle dit - ty in her good ould I - rish way, and I'd

give the world if she could sing that song to me this day.

AN IRISH LULLABY

Verse 2.
Oft in dreams I wander to that little cot again.
I feel her arms a-hugging me as when she held me then.
And I hear her voice a-humming to me as in days of yore,
When she used to rock me fast asleep outside the cabin door.
CHORUS

ARTHUR McBRIDE

Ukulele tuning: gCEA

Verse 1. Oh, me and my cous - in one Ar - thur Mc Bride as

we went a walk - ing down by the sea - side, --we -

met Ser - geant Nap - per and Cor - por - al Pride, the

day be - ing Christ - mas morn - ing. "Good

morn - ing, good morn - ing," the ser - geant he cried, "And the

same to you, gen - tle - men," we did re - ply. "In -

tend - ing no harm we just meant to pass by, the

day be - ing pleas - ant and charm - - - ing."

ARTHUR McBRIDE

Verse 2.
"But," says he, "my fine fellows, if you will enlist,
Ten guineas in gold I will slip in your fist,
And a crown in the bargain for to kick up the dust
And drink the King's health in the morning.
For a soldier he leads a very fine life,
And he always is blessed with a charming young wife,
While other poor fellows have sorrow and strife,
And sip on thin gruel in the morning."

Verse 3.
"But," says Arthur, "I wouldn't be proud of your clothes,
For you've only the lend of them, as I suppose;
And if you dare change them one night if you do,
You know you'll be flogged in the morning.
And we have no desire to take your advance,
For all of the dangers we'd not take a chance.
For you'd have no scrupples and send us to France
Where you know we'd be shot in the morning."

Verse 4.
"Oh, no," says the sergeant, "if I hear one more word,
I'll cut you right now and take out me sword,
And into your body as strength might afford,
And now, me young devils, take warning."
But Arthur and I we counted our odds
And we'd scarce give them time for to draw their own blades,
With our trusty shillelaghs we knocked in their heads,
And paid them right smart in the morning.

Verse 5.
And their rusty old rapiers that hung by their side,
We flung them as far as we could in the tide.
"Now, take that, you devils," cried Arthur McBride,
"And temper your steel in the morning."
And their little wee drummer, we flattened his pouch,
And we made a football of his rowdy-dow-dow,
We then threw it in the ocean for to rock and to roll,
And bade it a tedious returning.

Verse 6.
Oh, me and my cousin, one Arthur McBride,
As we went a-walking down by the seaside
A-seeking good fortune and what might betide,
It being on Christmas morning.

THE BAND PLAYED ON

Ukulele tuning: gCEA

JOHN F. PALMER

CHARLES B. WARD

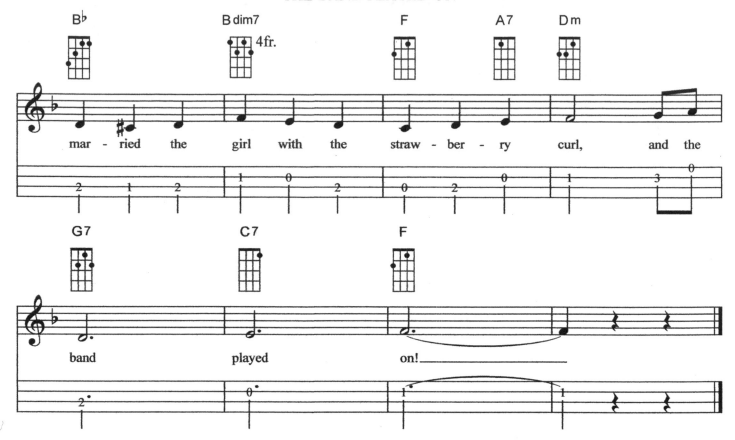

A LIMERICK

An Irishman name of McPheeny
In France drank a quart of Martini.
    The local gendarme
    Wired his wife in alarm,
"Nous regrettons, McPheeny est fini!"

BELIEVE ME
IF ALL THOSE ENDEARING YOUNG CHARMS

Ukulele tuning: gCEA

Considered to be Ireland's National Bard, Thomas Moore (1779-1852) is revered for his elegant poetry, an example of which we have both here and elsewhere in this book with the lyrics to "The Minstrel Boy." The familiar melody has been adopted by Harvard University for its alma mater.

THOMAS MOORE   **Traditional Air**

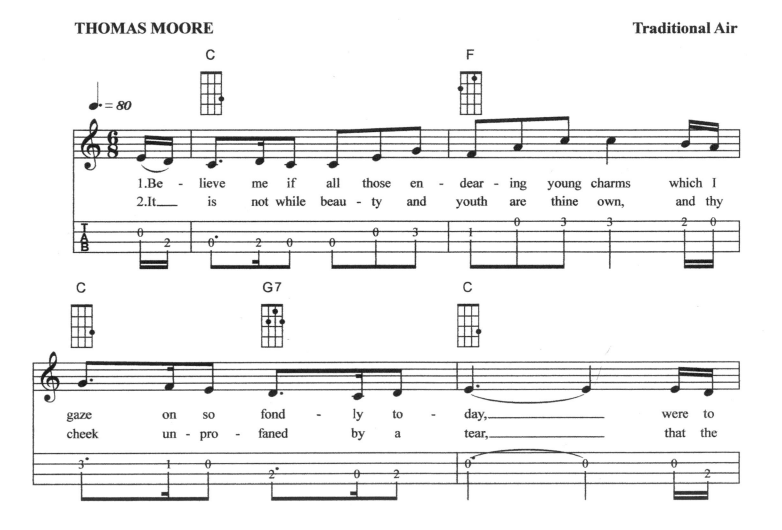

1.Be - lieve me if all those en - dear - ing young charms, which I
2.It___ is not while beau - ty and youth are thine own, and thy

gaze on so fond - ly to - day,_____ were to
cheek un - pro - faned by a tear,_____ that the

The longest road out is the shortest road home.
oOo

BELIEVE ME IF ALL THOSE ENDEARING YOUNG CHARMS

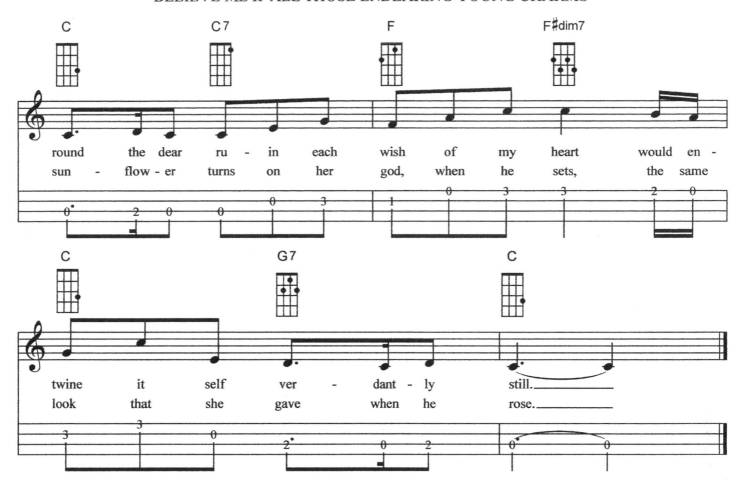

round   the   dear   ru - in   each   wish   of   my   heart   would   en -

sun - flow - er   turns   on   her   god,   when   he   sets,   the   same

twine   it   self   ver - dant - ly   still.

look   that   she   gave   when   he   rose.

Here's to you and yours, And to mine and ours,
And if mine and ours ever come across you and
yours, I hope you and yours will do as much for
mine and ours and mine and ours have done for
you and yours!

oOo

THE BLACK VELVET BAND

Ukulele tuning: gCEA

Traditional

Verse 2.
A watch she pulled out of her pocket,
And slipped it right into my hand,
On the very first day that I met her,
Bad luck to her black velvet band.

Verse 3.
Before judge and jury next morning,
The both of us had to appear;
A gentleman claimed his jewelry,
And the case against us was quite clear.

Verse 4.
Seven long years was the sentence,
I was sent down to Van Dieman's Land,
Far away from my friends and relations,
Betrayed by the black velvet band.

Verse 5.
Come all ye brave lads take a warning,
I'll have you take warning by me,
Beware of the pretty young damsels
You'll find on the streets of Tralee.

Verse 6.
They'll treat you to whiskey and porter
Until you're unable to stand,
And before you have time to regret it,
You'll be sent off to Van Dieman's Land.

Van Dieman's Land, referenced in this last verse, was a British penal colony from about 1800 to 1850. Convicts served out their sentences on the island of Tasmania, which is now part of Australia.

BRENNAN ON THE MOOR

Like Robin Hood, Willie Brennan supposedly took from the rich and gave to the poor. But his outlaw career ended with betrayal, and a sad fate awaited him on the gallows.

Ukulele tuning: gCEA

Traditional

Verse 1. Oh, it's of a bold young high-way man this sto-ry I will tell. His name was Wil-lie Bren-nan and in Ire-land he did dwell. 'Twas on the Kil-worth moun-tains he be-gan his wild ca-reer, where man-y a weal-thy gen-tle-man be-fore him shook with fear. Oh, it's

Chorus: Bren-nan on the moor, Bren-nan on the moor, bold, brave, and un-daunt-ed stood young Bren-nan on the moor.

Verse 2.
A brace of loaded pistols he carried night and day.
He never robbed a poor man upon the King's highway.
What he's taken from the rich, like Turpin and Black Bess,
He always did divide it with a widow in distress.
CHORUS

Verse 3.
One day upon the highway, as Willie he went down,
He met up with the Mayor five miles out of town.
The Mayor knew his features, "I think, young man" says he,
"Your name is Willie Brennan, you must come along with me."
CHORUS

Verse 4.
Now Willie's wife had gone to town, provisions for to buy,
But when she saw poor Willie she began to weep and cry.
He says, "Hand me that tenpenny," and as soon as Willie spoke,
She handed him a blunderbuss from underneath her cloak.
CHORUS

Verse 5.
Then with his loaded blunderbuss, the truth I will enfold,
He made the Mayor tremble, and he robbed him of his gold.
One hundred pounds was offered for his apprehension there,
So he with horse and saddle to the mountains did repair.
CHORUS

COCKLES AND MUSSELS

(Molly Malone)

Ukulele tuning: gCEA

Traditional

Verse 1. In Dub - lin's fair cit - y where the girls are so pret - ty I

first set my eyes on sweet Mol - ly Ma - lone, as she

wheeled her wheel - bar - row thru the streets broad and nar - row, cry - ing,

It is often that a person's mouth broke his nose.

oOo

Verse 2.
She was a fishmonger, and sure 'twas no wonder,
For her father and mother were fishmongers too,
And they both wheeled their barrow
Thru streets broad and narrow,
Crying, "Cockles and mussels, alive, alive, O!"
CHORUS

Verse 3.
She died of the fever, and no one could save her,
And that was the end of sweet Molly Malone.
Now her ghost wheels her barrow
Thru streets broad and narrow,
Crying, "Cockles and mussels, alive, alive, O!"
CHORUS

If you're an Irish tenor, or wish you were, you can be sure this is one song you'll always be requested to sing. And when you hit that high G on the 10th fret, the glasses will shatter, the dishes will rattle, and there won't be a dry eye in the house.

DANNY BOY

Ukulele tuning: gCEA

MUSIC:
To the tune of "Londonderry Air"

FREDERIC WEATHERLY

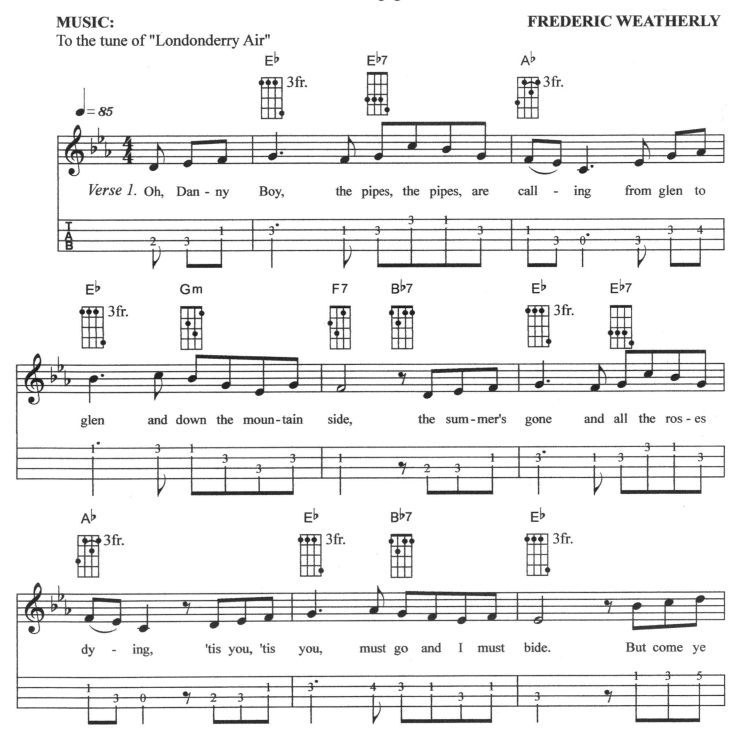

Verse 2.
And when you come and all the flowers are dying,
If I am dead, as dead I well may be,
Ye'll come and find a place where I am lying
And kneel and say an Ave there for me.
And I shall hear, though soft your tread above me,
And all my grave shall warmer, sweeter be,
For you will bend and tell me that you love me,
And I shall live in peace until you come to me.

Dicey Riley

Ukulele tuning: gCEA

Traditional

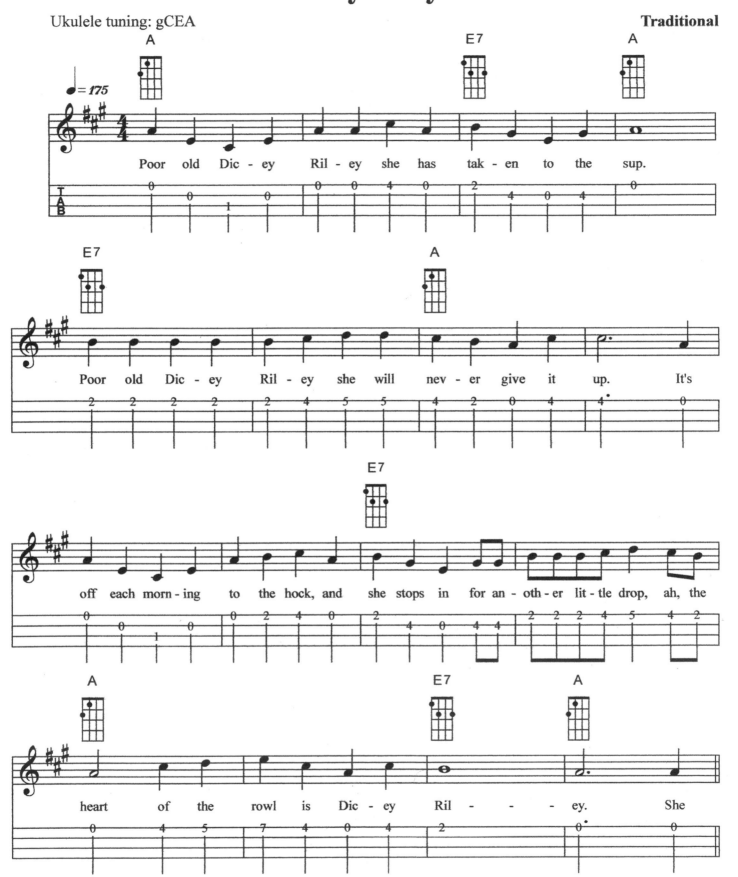

Poor old Dic - ey Ril - ey she has tak - en to the sup.

Poor old Dic - ey Ril - ey she will nev - er give it up. It's

off each morn - ing to the hock, and she stops in for an - oth - er lit - tle drop, ah, the

heart of the rowl is Dic - ey Ril - - - ey. She

Dicey Riley

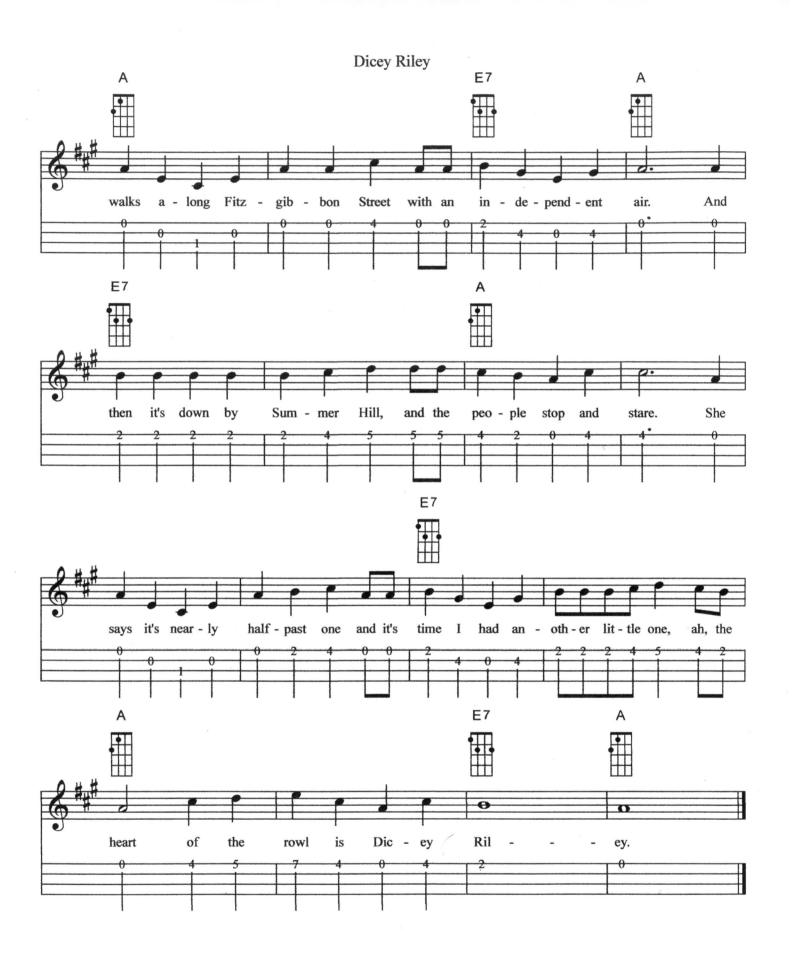

DO YOU WANT YOUR OLD LOBBY WASHED DOWN

Ukulele tuning: gCEA

Traditional

Verse 1. I've a nice little cot and a small bit of land, and a place by the side of the sea. And I care about no-one be-cause I believe there's no-body cares a-about me. My peace is de-stroyed and I'm fair-ly an-noyed by a las-sie who works in the

DO YOU WANT YOUR OLD LOBBY WASHED DOWN

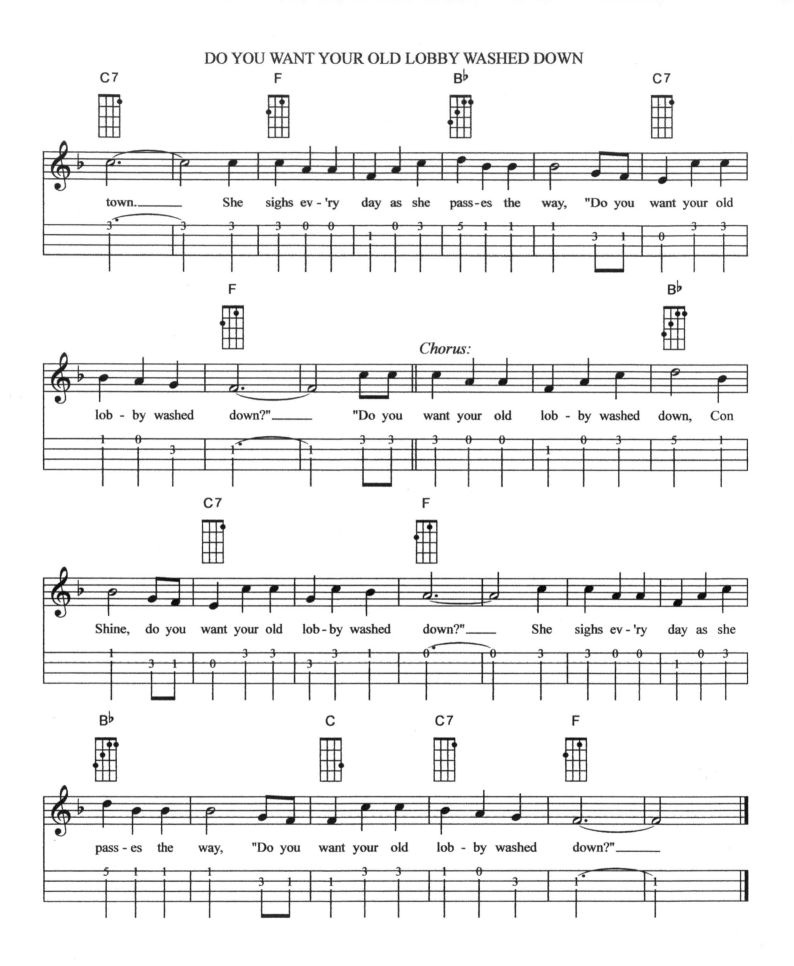

town._____ She sighs ev-'ry day as she pass-es the way, "Do you want your old

lob-by washed down?"_____ "Do you want your old lob-by washed down, Con

Chorus:

Shine, do you want your old lob-by washed down?"_____ She sighs ev-'ry day as she

pass-es the way, "Do you want your old lob-by washed down?"_____

Verse 2.
The other day the old landlord came by for his rent,
I told him no money I had;
Besides 'twasn't fair for to ask me to pay,
The times were so awfully bad.
He felt discontent at not getting his rent,
And he shook his big head in a frown.
Says he, "I'll take half," but says I with a laugh,
"Do you want your old lobby washed down?"
CHORUS

Verse 3.
Now the boys look so bashful when they go out courting,
They seem to look so very shy.
As to kiss a young maid, sure, they seem half afraid,
But they would if they could on the sly.
But me, I do things in a different way,
I don't give a nod or a frown,
When I go to court, I says, "Here goes for sport,
Do you want your old lobby washed down?"
CHORUS

FOGGY DEW

Ukulele tuning: gCEA

CANON CHARLES O'NEILL

Verse 2.
Right proudly high over Dublin Town they hung out the flag of war,
'Twas better to die 'neath an Irish sky than at Suvla or Sud-El-Bar.
And from the plains of Royal Meath strong men came hurrying through,
While Britannia's Huns with their long-range guns sailed in through the foggy dew.

Verse 3.
Oh the night fell black and the rifles' crack made perfidious Albion reel,
In the leaden rain seven tongues of flame did shine o'er the lines of steel.
By each shining blade a prayer was said that to Ireland her sons be true,
But when morning broke still the war flag shook out its folds in the foggy dew.

Verse 4.
'Twas England bade our wild geese go that "small nations might be free;"
Their lonely graves are by Suvla's waves or the fringe of the great North Sea.
Oh, had they died by Pearse's side or fought with Valera true,
Their graves we'd keep where the Fenians sleep 'neath the shroud of the foggy dew.

Verse 5.
Oh, the bravest fell and the requiem bell rang mournfully and clear
For those who died that Eastertide in the springtime of the year.
And the world did gaze in deep amaze at those fearless men, but few,
Who bore the fight that freedom's light might shine through the foggy dew.

Verse 6.
As back through the glen I rode again and my heart with grief was sore,
For I parted then with valiant men whom I never shall see no more.
But to and fro in my dreams I go, and I kneel and I pray for you,
For slavery fled, O glorious dead, when you fell in the foggy dew.

Commemorated here in song is the lamented unsuccessful Irish rebellion from British rule known as the Easter Rising of 1916. A number of references in the song bear explanation:

LIFFEY = a river that runs through the center of Dublin.
SULVA and SUD-EL-BAR = locations in Turkey on the Aegean Coast, scenes of British fighting in World War I during the Battle of Gallipoli.
ROYAL MEATH = a nickname for County Meath in the north of Ireland.
ALBION = the Greek name for Great Britian, referred to as perfidious, treacherous.
WILD GEESE = Irish mercenaries who fought in various European armies.
PEARSE = Patrick Pearse, an Irish nationalist executed by the British for his particpation in the Easter Uprising.
VALERA = Eamon de Valera, a political activist for Irish independence.
FENIANS = an organization dedicated to an independent Irish Republic.

GARRY OWEN

An Irish "quickstep" march, long a favorite of military and civilian marching bands. Its history
precedes the Civil War and is currently the official march of the US 1st Cavalry Division.

Ukulele tuning: gCEA

Traditional

HARRIGAN

Ukulele tuning: gCEA

GEORGE M. COHAN

Verse 1. Who is the man who will spend or will ev-en lend? Har-ri-gan, that's me!

Who is your friend when you find that you need a friend? Har-ri-gan, that's me! For

I'm just as proud of my name, you see, as an Em-per-or, Czar, or a King could be.

Who is the man helps a man ev-'ry time he can? Har-ri-gan, that's me!

HARRIGAN

Verse 2. Who is the man never stood for a gadabout? Harrigan, that's me!
Who is the man that the town's simply mad about? Harrigan, that's me!
The ladies and babies are fond of me, I'm fond of them, too, in return, you see.
Who is the gent that's deserving a monument? Harrigan, that's me!
CHORUS

THE HILLS OF CONNEMARA

"Mountain tay" -- Irish moonshine, the equivalent of our own "good old mountain dew."

Ukulele tuning: gCEA

Traditional

Gath - er up the pots and the old tin cans, the mash, the corn, the bar - ley and the bran, run like the dev - il from the ex - cise man, keep the smoke from ris - ing, Bar - ney!

Verse 2. Keep your eyes well peeled today, the tall, tall men are on their way,
Searching for the mountain tay, in the hills of Connemara.

Verse 3. Swing to the left and swing to the right, the excise men will dance all night,
Drinking up the tay till the broad daylight, in the hills of Connemara.

Verse 4. A gallon for the butcher, a quart for Tom, a bottle for poor old Father Tom,
To help the poor old dear along, in the hills of Connemara.

Verse 5. Stand your ground, it is too late, the excise men are at the gate,
Glory be to Paddy but they're drinking it nate, in the hills of Connemara.

IF YOU'RE IRISH, COME INTO THE PARLOR

Ukulele tuning: gCEA

Words & Music by
FRANK MILLER & SHAUN GLENVILLE

If you're I - rish,_____ come in - to the par - - - lor, there's a

wel - come there for you._____ If your

name is Tim - o - thy or Pat_____ so

long as you come from Ire - land there's a "wel - come" on the mat. If you

I'LL TAKE YOU HOME AGAIN, KATHLEEN

Ukulele tuning: gCEA

THOMAS P. WESTENDORF

I'LL TAKE YOU HOME AGAIN, KATHLEEN

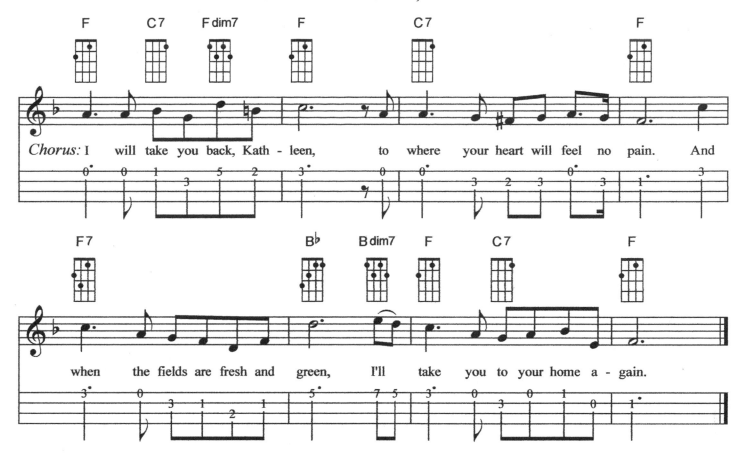

Verse 2.
I know you love me, Kathleen, dear,
Your heart was ever fond and true.
I always feel when you are near
That life holds nothing, dear, but you.
The smiles that once you gave to me,
I scarcely ever see them now,
Though many, many times I see
A dark'ning shadow on your brow.
Chorus

Verse 3.
To that dear home beyond the sea,
My Kathleen shall again return.
And when thy old friends welcome thee,
Thy loving heart will cease to yearn.
Where laughs the little silver stream
Beside your mother's humble cot,
And brightest rays of sunshine gleam,
There all your grief will be forgot.
Chorus

I'll Tell Me Ma

Ukulele Tuning: gCEA

Traditional

Verse 2.
Albert Mooney says he loves her,
All the boys are fighting for her,
They knock at the door, and they ring at the bell,
Saying, "Oh, my true love, are you well?"
Out she comes as white as snow,
Rings on her fingers and bells on her toes;
Old Johnny Murray says she'll die
If she doesn't get the fellow with the roving eye.

Verse 3.
Let the wind and the rain and the hail blow high,
And the snow come tumbling from the sky.
She's as nice as apple pie,
She'll get her own lad by and by.
When she gets a lad of her own,
She won't tell her ma when she goes home.
Let them all come as they will,
It's Albert Mooney she loves still.

I MET HER IN THE GARDEN

Ukulele tuning: gCEA

JOHNNY PATTERSON

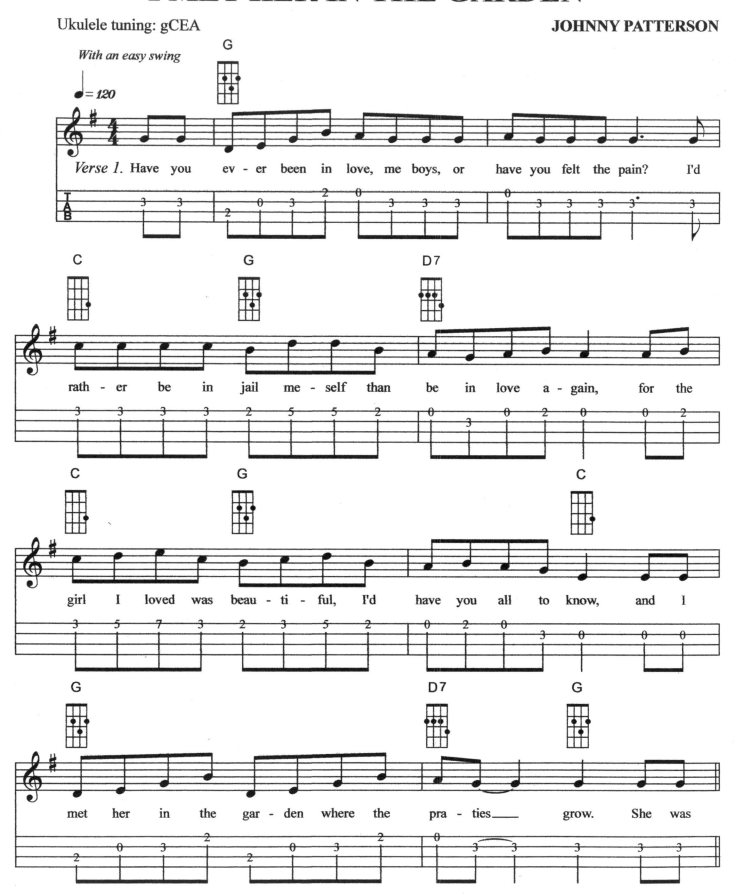

I MET HER IN THE GARDEN

Chorus: just the kind of crea - ture, boys, that na - ture did in - tend to walk right through the world, me boys, with - out the Gre - cian Bend. Nor did she wear a chi - gnon___ I'd have you all to know, and I met her in the gar - den where the pra - ties___ grow.

"Grecian Bend" -- We are all slaves to fashion, and certainly the ladies of the mid-1860s were no exception. The Grecian Bend was a bustle, a posterior caboose, if you will, that attached to a corset and protuded in the back below the waist. The chignon, which is a knot of hair at the back of the head, still remains fashionable.

Verse 2.
Says I, "Me pretty Kathleen, I'm tired of single life,
And if you've no objection, sure, I'll make you my sweet wife."
She answered me right modestly, and courtsied very low,
"Sure, you're welcome in the garden where the praties grow."
CHORUS

Verse 3.
Says I, "Me pretty Kathleen, I hope that you'll agree."
She wasn't like the city girls that say, "You're making free."
She says, "I'll ask my parents and tomorrow I'll let you know,
If you'll meet me in the garden where the praties grow."
CHORUS

Verse 4.
Oh, the parents they consented, and we're blessed with children three:
Two boys just like their mother, and a girl the image of me.
And now we're going to bring them up the way they ought to go,
For to dig in the garden where the praties grow.
CHORUS

THE IRISH ROVER

Verse 2.
We had one million bags of the best Sligo rags,
We had two million barrels of bone,
We had three million bales of old nanny goats' tails,
We had four million barrels of stone.
We had five million hogs and six million dogs,
And seven million barrels of porter,
We had eight million sides of old horses' hides,
In the hold of the Irish Rover.

Only Irish coffee provides in a single glass all four essential food groups: alcohol, caffeine, sugar, and fat.

~~By Alex Levine.~~

IRISH WASHERWOMAN

Ukulele tuning: gCEA

Traditional

THE KERRY DANCE

Ukulele tuning: gCEA

JAMES LYNAM MOLLOY

THE KERRY DANCE

THE LITTLE BEGGARMAN

Because of the range of this tune and the limited range of the ukulele, a few adjustments were made to the melody although its essence has been carefully preserved. The tiny 3s indicate "triplets," that is, three notes on one beat, counted as "triple it." These reflect the ornamentation commonly used by players of traditional Irish music.

Ukulele tuning: gCEA

Traditional Irish tune

LITTLE TOWN IN THE OULD COUNTY DOWN

Ukulele tuning: gCEA

RICHARD W. PASCOE　　　　　　　　　**MONTE CARLO & ALMA SANDERS**

McNAMARA'S BAND

Ukulele tuning: gCEA

JOHN J. STAMFORD

SHAMUS O'CONNOR

Verse 1. Oh, me name is Mc Na - mar - a, I'm the lead - er of the band,____ al -

though we're few in num - bers, we're the fin - est in the land. We

play at wakes and wed - dings and at ev - 'ry fan - cy ball,____ and

when we play to fun - er - als we play the march from "Saul." Oh, the

Note: "Saul" was an oratorio written by George Frideric Handel that included a solemn "dead march" funeral anthem.

McNAMARA'S BAND

*Our school librarian referred to a classmate as Mr. McNAM-a-ra, and perhaps that's the
way some Irish might pronounce the name. But whatever the proper pronunciation, there's
no confusion about the popularity of the song. It's unquestionably the favorite of almost every
marching band in every St. Patrick's Day parade. The lively beat can't be denied, and the lyrics
are just too much fun not to be sung.*

Instrumental:

Verse 2.
Right now we are rehearsin' for a very swell affair,
The annual celebration, all the gentry will be there.
When Gen'ral Grant to Ireland came, he shook me by the hand,
Says he, "I never saw the likes of McNamara's Band."
CHORUS

Verse 3.
Oh, my name is Uncle Yulius and from Sweden I have come,
To play with McNamara's Band and beat the big bass drum.
And when I march along the street, the ladies think I'm grand,
They shout, "There's Uncle Yulius playing with an Irish band."
(NO CHORUS)

Verse 4.
Oh, I wear a bunch of shamrocks and a uniform of green,
And I'm the funniest looking Swede that you have ever seen.
There's O'Briens & Ryans & Sheehans & Meehans, they come from Ireland,
But by jimminy I'm the only Swede in McNamara's Band.
CHORUS and INSTRUMENTAL

THE MERMAID

Mariners are a superstitious lot, and the sight of a mermaid was thought to be an ill omen. Strictly speaking, this sea shanty might not be considered Irish, although it is certainly popular with Irish singing groups, the Clancy Brothers among the many.

Ukulele tuning: gCEA

Traditional

Verse 1. 'Twas Fri-day morn when we set sail, and we were not far from land. When the cap-tain spied a pret-ty mer-maid with a comb and a glass in her hand. Oh, the

Chorus: o - cean waves may roll, let 'em roll, and the storm - y winds may blow, but

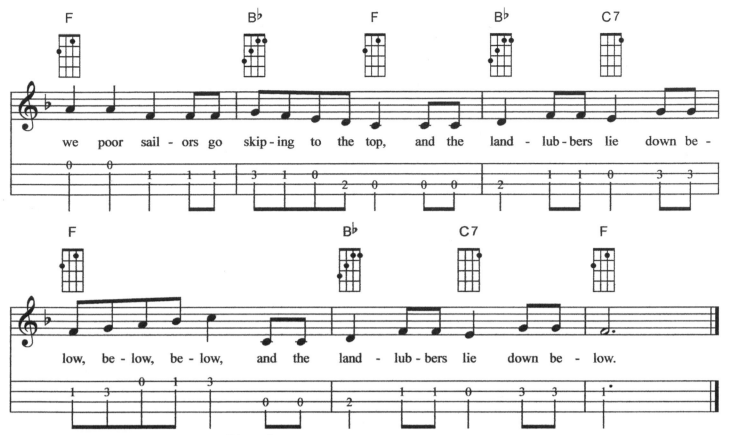

Verse 2.
Then up spoke the captain of our gallant ship,
And a well-spoken man was he.
"I have me a wife in Salem town,
And tonight a widow she will be."
CHORUS

Verse 3.
Then up spoke the cook of our gallant ship,
And a right good cook was he.
"I care more for my pots and my pans,
Than I do for the bottom of the sea."
CHORUS

Verse 3.
Then up spoke the cabin-boy of our gallant ship,
And a dirty little rat was he.
"There's nary a soul in Salem town
Who will give a darn about me."
CHORUS

Verse 4.
Then three times around went our gallant ship,
And three times around went she.
Three times around went our gallant ship,
And she sank to the bottom of the sea.
CHORUS

THE MERRY PLOWBOY

Ukulele tuning: gCEA

Traditional

Verse 1. Oh, I am a mer-ry plow-boy, and I plow the fields all day, till a sud - den thought came to my mind that I should run a - way. Well, I'm sick and tired of slav - 'ry since the day that I was born, so I'm off to join the I. R. A., I'll be gone to - mor - row morn. Well, I'm

Chorus: off to Dub-lin in the green, in the green, where the hel-mets glis-ten in the sun, where the bay-o-nets flash, and the ri-fles clash to the ech-o of a Thomp-son gun.

Verse 2.
I'll leave aside my pick and spade,
And I'll leave aside my plow,
I'll leave aside my old grey mare
For no more I'll need them now.
And I'll leave aside my Mary,
She's the girl that I adore,
And I wonder if she'll think of me
When she hears the canons roar.
CHORUS

Verse 3.
(Last 8 bars)
And when this war is over,
And dear old Ireland's free,
I'll take her to the church to wed,
And a rebel's wife she'll be.
CHORUS

THE MINSTREL BOY

Ukulele tuning: gCEA

THOMAS MOORE

Ancient Irish Air

Verse 2.
The Minstrel fell! but the foeman's chain
Could not bring that proud soul under.
The harp he lov'd ne'er spoke again,
For he tore its chords asunder.
And said "No chains shall sully thee,
Thou soul of love and brave'ry!
Thy songs were made for the pure and free,
They shall never sound in slavery!"

MISS McLEOD'S REEL

Originally a Scottish tune but now a standard in the Irish "sessions" repertoire.

Ukulele tuning: gCEA

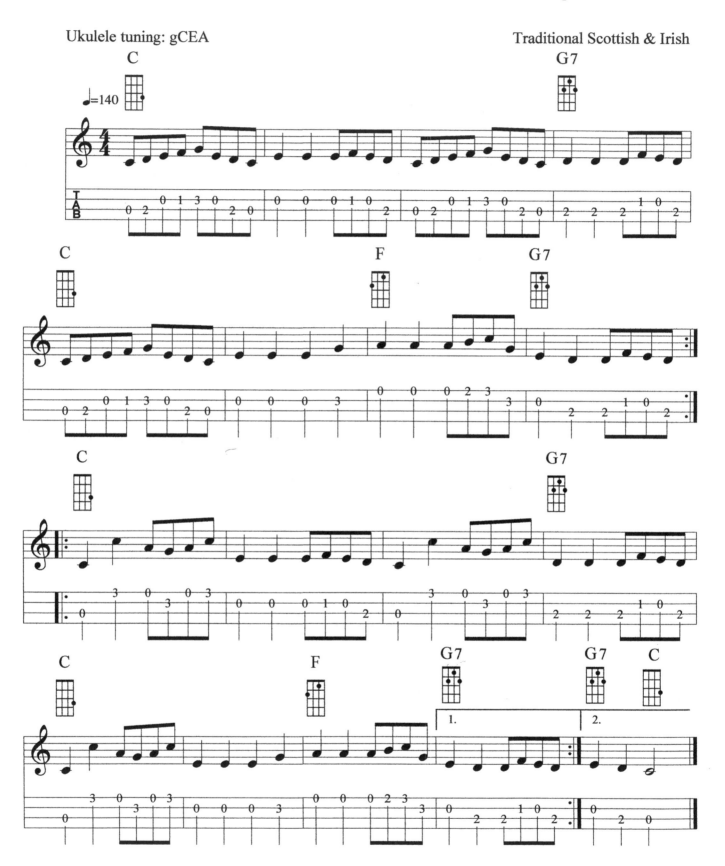

Traditional Scottish & Irish

MOTHER MACHREE

Ukulele tuning: gCEA

RIDA JOHNSON YOUNG

CHAUNCEY OLCOTT

MOTHER MACHREE

Verse 2.
Ev'ry sorrow or care in the dear days gone by
Was made bright by the light of the smile in your eye;
Like a candle that's set in the window at night,
Your fond love has cheered me and guided me right.
CHORUS

THE MOUTAINS O' MOURNE

PERCY FRENCH &
HOUSTON COLLISSON

Ukulele tuning: gCEA

THE MOUTAINS O' MOURNE

least when I axed them that's what I was told, so I just took a hand at this dig - gin' for gold. But for all that I found there I might as well be where the Moun - tains o' Mourne sweep down to the sea.

Verse 2.

I believe that when writin' a wish you expressed
As to how the fine ladies in London were dressed.
Well, if you'll believe me, when axed to a ball,
Faith, they don't wear a top to their dresses at all.
Oh, I've seen them meself, and you could not in thrath,
Say if they were bound for a ball or a bath.
Don't be startin' them fashions now, Mary Macree,
Where the Mountains o' Mourne sweep down to the sea.

Verse 3.

I've seen England's King from the top of a bus,
I never knew him, tho' he means to know us.
And tho' by the Saxon we once were oppressed,
Still, I cheered (God forgive me), I cheered wid the rest.
And now that he's visited Erin's green shore,
We'll be much better friends than we've been here tofore.
When we've got all we want, we're quiet as can be,
Where the Mountains o' Mourne sweep down to the sea.

Verse 4.

You remember young Peter O'Loughlin, of course,
Well, now he is here at the head o' the force;
I met him today, I was crossin' the Strand,
And he stopped the whole street wid wan wave of his hand.
And there we stood talkin' of days that are gone,
While the whole population of London looked on.
But for all these great powers he's wishful like me
To be back where dark Mourne sweeps down to the sea.

Verse 5.

There's beautiful girls here, Oh! niver mind!
Wid beautiful shapes Nature niver designed,
And lovely complexions all roses and creme.
But O'Loughlin remarked wid regard to the same
That if at those roses you venture to sip
The colors might all come away on your lip.
So I'll wait for the wild rose that's waitin' for me,
Where the Mountains o' Mourne sweep down to the sea.

WHO THREW THE OVERALLS
IN MRS. MURPHY'S CHOWDER?

Ukulele tuning: gCEA

GEORGE L. GIEFER

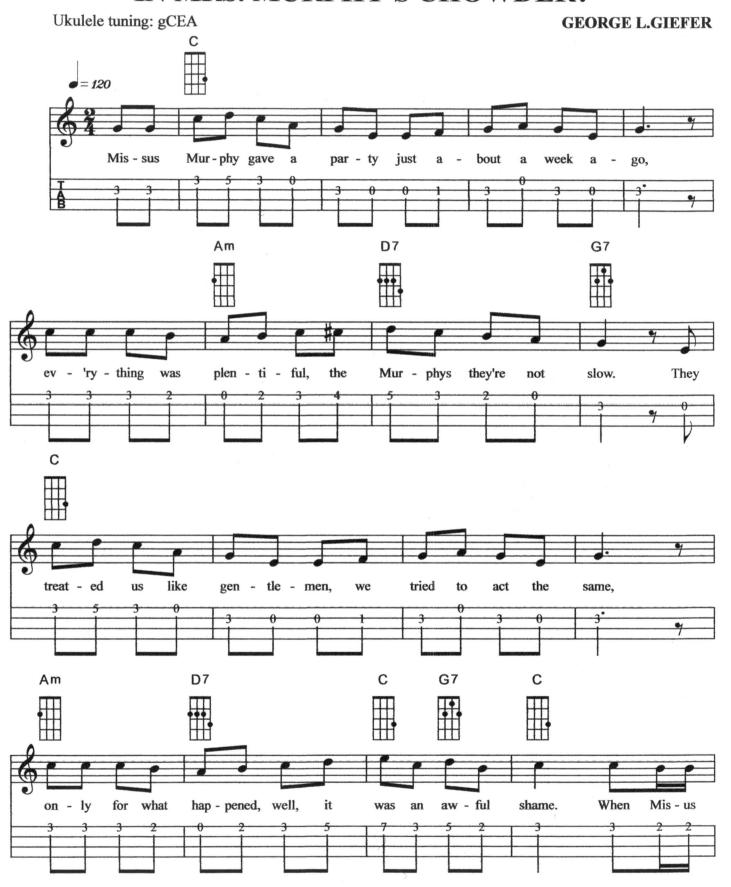

Mur - phy dished the chow - der out, she faint - ed on the spot, she

found a pair of o - ver - alls at the bot - tom of the pot. Tim

No - lan he got rip - ping mad, his eyes were bulg - ing out, he

jumped up on the pi - an - o and loud - ly he did shout:

THE MULLIGAN GUARD

Ukulele tuning: gCEA

EDWARD HARRIGAN   **DAVID BRAHAM**

THE MULLIGAN GUARD

Verse 2.
When the band play'd Garry Owen,
Or the Connamara Pet;
With a rub-a-dub-dub, we'd march in the mud
To the military step.
With the green above the red, boys,
To show where we come from,
Our guns we'd lift with the right shoulder shift
As we'd march to the beat of the drum.
CHORUS

Verse 3.
When we got home at night, boys,
The devil a bite we'd ate,
We'd all set up and drink a sup
Of whiskey strong and nate.
Then we'd all march home together,
As slippery as lard,
The solid men would all fall in
And march with the Mulligan Guard.
CHORUS

HARRIGAN & HART

Edward (Ned) Harrigan and Tony Hart formed the celebrated team of "Harrigan & Hart" considered to be the first two-man comedy collaboration in the American musical theater. Their vaudeville sketch of "The Mulligan Guard" proved so successful that it became the springboard for a series of full-length comedies set to the music of Harrigan's future father-in-law David Braham. The shows depicted street life in lower Manhattan with good-natured spoofs directed at a lower and middle class multi-national population, many of whom were, of course, Irish immigrants. Part of the fun was portrayal of neighborhood marching bands, called guards, which in reality were nothing more than uniformed drinking clubs. Besides performing in all these productions, Harrigan also wrote, directed, and produced them. Lasting tribute has been paid to him by George M. Cohan in his popular song "Harrigan" with its unforgettable letter lyrics, "H-A-double R-I-G-A-N spells Harrigan ..."

MY IRISH MOLLY O

Ukulele tuning: gCEA

WILLIAM JEROME   **JEAN SCHWARTZ**

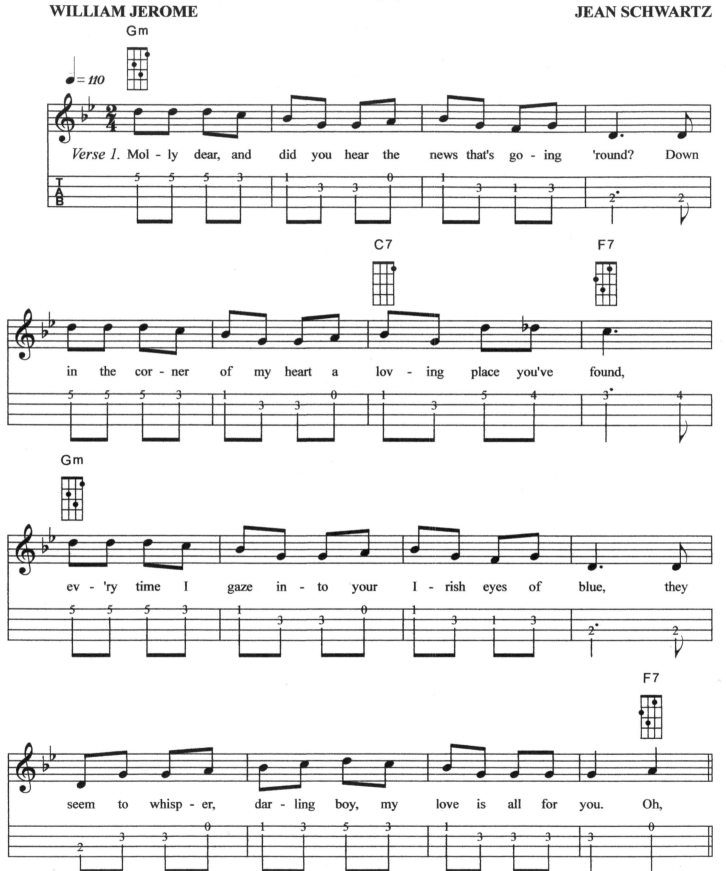

MY IRISH MOLLY O

Verse 2. Molly dear, and did you hear, I furnished up the flat,
Three little cozy rooms and bath, and "Welcome" on the mat.
It's five pounds down and two a week, we'll soon be out of debt,
It's all complete except we haven't bought a cradle yet.
CHORUS

Verse 3. Molly dear, and did you hear what all the neighbors say,
About the hundred sovereigns you have safely stowed away?
They say that's why I love you, ah, but Molly that's a shame,
If you had only ninety-nine I'd love you just the same.
CHORUS

Maybe it's bred in the bone, but the sound of pipes is a little bit of heaven to some of us.

~~By Nancy O'Keeefe.~~

MY LAGAN LOVE

Ukulele tuning: gCEA

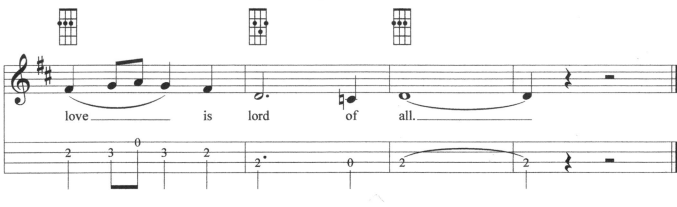

Verse 2.
And often when the beetle's horn
Hath lulled the eve to sleep,
I steal unto her shieling lorn
And through the dooring peep.
There on the cricket's singing stone,
She spares the bogwood fire
And hums in sad sweet undertone
The songs of heart's desire.

Verse 3.
Her welcome, like her love for me,
Is from her heart within;
Her warm kiss is felicity
That knows no taint of sin.
And when I stir my foot to go,
'Tis leaving love and light
To feel the wind of longing blow
From out the dark of night.

"For Love Is Lord Of All"

"My Lagan Love" is one of the most hauntingly beautiful of all Irish ballads.
The reference to "Lagan stream" appears to be a river that flows through
Belfast, but other locations have been suggested. The term "lennan-shee"
is Gaelic and refers to a mythical malevolent fairy who entices men to fall
in love with her and then abandons them to pine away in fatal love sickness.

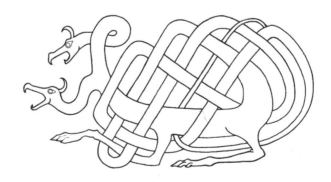

MY WILD IRISH ROSE

Ukulele tuning: gCEA

CHAUNCEY OLCOTT

NELLIE KELLY

Ukulele tuning: gCEA

GEORGE M. COHAN

PADDY WORKS ON THE RAILWAY

Ukulele tuning: gCEA

Traditional

Verse 2.
In eighteen hundred and forty-two,
I didn't know what I was going to do (2x),
Working on the railway.
CHORUS

Verse 3.
In eighteen hundred and forty-three,
The section boss kept driving me (2x), etc.

Verse 4.
In eighteen hundred and forty-four,
My hands and feet were getting sore (2x), etc.

Verse 5.
In eighteen hundred and forty-five,
Found myself more dead than alive (2x), etc.

Verse 6.
In eighteen hundred and forty-six,
I made my living by carrying bricks (2x), etc.

Verse 7.
In eighteen hundred and forty-seven,
Paddy was off on his way to heaven (2x), etc.

Verse 8.
In eighteen hundred and forty-eight,
Paddy drank his whiskey straight (2x), etc.

Verse 9.
In eighteen hundred and forty-nine,
Paddy reached the end of the line (2x), etc.

Verse 10.
In eighteen hundred and forty-ten,
Paddy was back on the earth again (2x), etc.

Irish immigrants fresh off the boat took what jobs they could find, and these were often as laborers, tradesmen, construction workers, canal diggers, and railroad "gandy dancers." Paddy's toil is typical of the harsh demands of the time required to eke out even a subsistence living. But his efforts along with those of others like him are recalled with a pinch of good humor in this fun song. It's a great one for singing around a campfire, at a cookout, wherever, with a leader bellowing out the verses and a group coming in with a rousing chorus.

PEG O' MY HEART

Ukulele tuning: gCEA

FRED FISCHER

come, make my home_____ in your heart._____

It's days like this when I wish I played the ukulele.

THE RISING OF THE MOON

Ukulele tuning: gCEA

Words by
JOHN KEEGAN CASEY

Traditional Tune
"Wearing Of The Green"

Note: "ma bouchal" are Irish words for "my boy."

THE RISING OF THE MOON

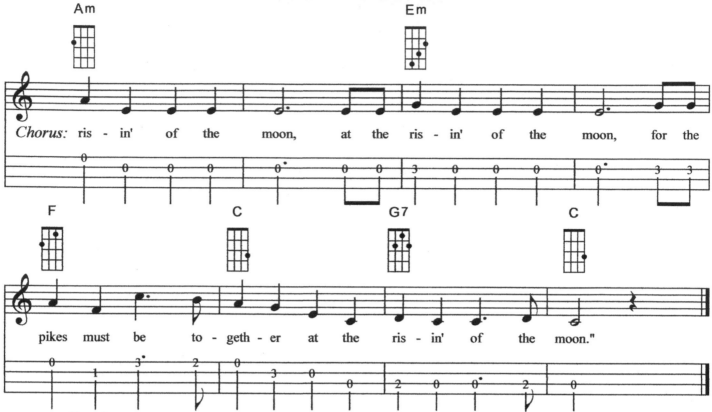

Am   **Em**

Chorus: ris - in'   of   the   moon,   at   the   ris - in'   of   the   moon,   for   the

F   **C**   **G7**   **C**

pikes   must   be   to - geth - er   at   the   ris - in'   of   the   moon."

Verse 2.

"Oh then, tell me Sean O'Farrell, where the gatherin' is to be?"
"In the old spot by the river right well known to you and me.
One word more: for signal token, whistle up the marching tune,
With your pike upon your shoulder, by the risin' of the moon."
CHORUS
"By the risin' of the moon, by the risin' of the moon,
With your pike upon your shoulder, by the risin' of the moon."

Verse 3.

Out from many a mud wall cabin eyes were watching through the night,
Many a manly heart was throbbing for the blessed warning light.
Murmurs passed along the valleys like the *banshee's lonely croon,
And a thousand blades were flashing at the risin' of the moon.
CHORUS
At the risin' of the moon, at the risin' of the moon,
And a thousand blades were flashing at the risin' of the moon.

*Banshee: an Irish ghost-like spirit whose wailing is said to be the herald of death.

Verse 4.

There beside the singing river that dark mass of men were seen,
Far above their shining weapons hung their own beloved green.
"Death to every foe and traitor! Forward! Strike the marching tune,
And hurrah, my boys, for freedom, 'tis the risin' of the moon!"
CHORUS
"'Tis the risin' of the moon, 'Tis the risin' of the moon,
And hurrah, my boys, for freedom, 'tis the risin' of the moon!"

Verse 5.

Well they fought for poor old Ireland, and full bitter was their fate.
(O, what glorious pride and sorrow fills the name of *Ninety-Eight!)
Yet, thank God, e'en still are beating hearts in manhood's burning noon,
Who would follow in their footsteps at the risin' of the moon.
CHORUS
"'Tis the risin' of the moon, 'tis the risin' of the moon,
And hurrah, my boys, for freedom, 'tis the risin' of the moon!"

*Ninety-eight: the Irish Rebellion of 1798. An unsuccessful attempt at freedom from British rule.

THE ROSE OF TRALEE

Ukulele tuning: gCEA

C. MORDAUNT SPENCER   **CHARLES W. GLOVER**

THE ROSE OF TRALEE

Verse 2. The cool shades of evening their mantle was spreading,
And Mary all smiling was list'ning to me.
The moon through the valley her pale rays was shedding
When I won the heart of the rose of Tralee.
CHORUS

SALLY GARDENS

Ukulele tuning: gCEA

From a poem by
WILLIAM BUTLER YEATS

HERBERT HUGHES

It was down by the Sal - ly Gar - dens my love and I did meet. She

passed the Sal - ly Gar - dens with lit - tle snow - white feet. She

bid me take love ea - sy as the leaves grow up on the tree. But

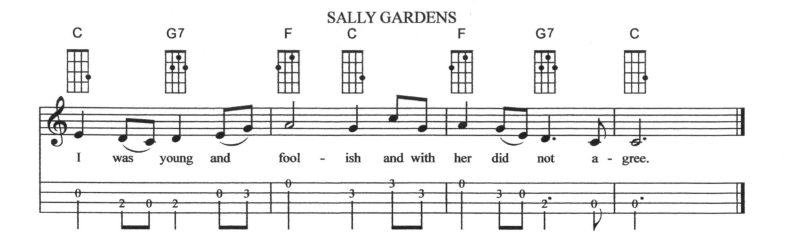

I was young and fool - ish and with her did not a - gree.

Verse 2.
In a field by the river my love and I did stand,
And on my leaning shoulder, she laid her snow-white hand.
She bid me take life easy, as the grass grows on the weirs,
But I was young and foolish, and now am full of tears.

Yeats claimed that his inspiration for the poem was from the singing of an elderly peasant woman from County Sligo who could vaguely remember only a few lines from an old song. That song was most certainly "The Rambling Boys Of Pleasure" whose opening lines are almost identical to those of Yeats' poem. Yeats, in fact, originally entitled his poem "An Old Song Re-Sung." The word "sally" is probably a variation of the Irish word for "willow," and Sally Gardens suggests a grove of such trees. Willows were used in Ireland for thatching material.

SPANCIL HILL

Ukulele tuning: gCEA

Traditional

Verse 1. Last night as I lay dream - - - ing of pleas - ant days gone by._____ Me mind been bent on ram - - - bling to Ire - land I did fly._____ I stepped on board a vi -

SPANCIL HILL

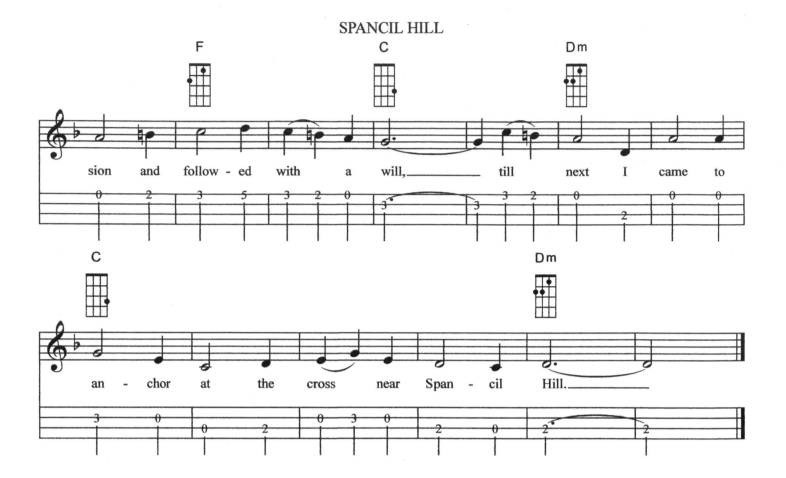

sion and follow - ed with a will,_____ till next I came to
an - chor at the cross near Span - cil Hill._____

Verse 2. It was on the twenty-third of June, the day before the fair,
When Ireland's sons and daughters were all assembled there,
The young, the old, the brave and bold, they came with bright goodwill,
To join in conversation at the cross of Spancil Hill.

Verse 3. I went to see my neighbors, to hear what they would say,
The old ones they were dead and gone, the young ones turning grey.
I met with the tailor Quigley, he's as bold as ever still,
He used to make my britches when I lived at Spancil Hill.

Verse 4. I paid a flying visit to my first and only love,
She's fair as any lily, and she's gentle as a dove.
She threw her arms around me saying, "Johnny, I love you still!"
She was the farmer's daughter and the pride of Spancil Hill.

Verse 5. I dreamt I hugged and kissed her as in the days of yore,
She said, "You're only joking as many's the time before."
The cock crew in the morning, he crew both loud and shrill,
And I woke in California many miles from Spancil Hill.

THE STAR OF THE COUNTY DOWN

Ukulele tuning: gCEA

Traditional

Verse 2.
She looked so sweet from her two bare feet,
To the sheen of her nut-brown hair,
Such a coaxing elf, sure I shook myself
For to see I was really there.
CHORUS

Verse 3.
As she onward sped, sure I scratched my head,
And I looked with a feeling rare,
And I says, says I, to a passer-by,
"Who's the maid with the nut-brown hair?"

Verse 4.
He smiled at me and he says, says he,
"That's the gem of Ireland's crown,
Young Rosie McCann from the banks of the Bann,
She's the star of the County Down."
CHORUS

Verse 5.
At the harvest fair, she'll be surely there,
So I dress in my Sunday clothes,
With my shoes shone bright and my hat cocked right,
For a smile from my nut-brown rose.

Verse 6.
No pipe I'll smoke, no horse I'll yoke,
Till my plow is a rust-colored brown,
Till a smiling bride by my own fireside,
Sits the star of the County Down.
CHORUS

SWALLOW TAIL JIG

Ukulele tuning: gCEA

Traditional Irish tune

SWEET ROSIE O'GRADY

Ukulele tuning: gCEA

MAUD NUGENT

THE WAXIES' DARGLE

Ukulele tuning: gCEA

Traditional

Verse 1. Says my old one to your old one "Will you come to the Wax - ies Dar - gle?" Says

my old one to your old one "Sure, I have - n't got a far - thing. I've

just been down to Mon - to town to see Un - cle Mc Ar - dle, but he

would - n't lend me half a crown for to go to the Wax - ies' Dar - gle." What

THE WAXIES' DARGLE

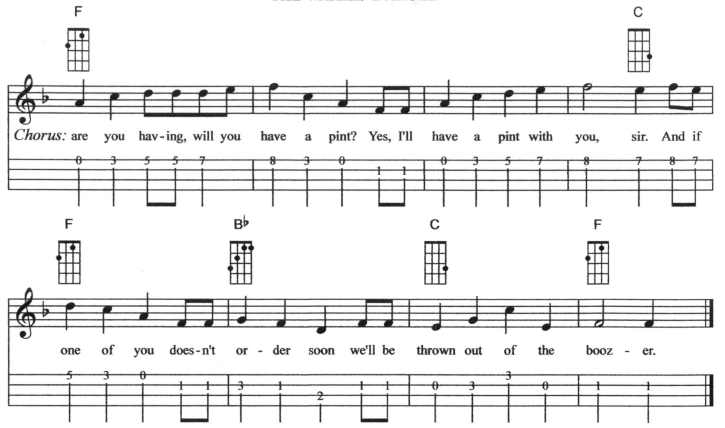

Chorus: are you hav-ing, will you have a pint? Yes, I'll have a pint with you, sir. And if one of you does-n't or - der soon we'll be thrown out of the booz - er.

Verse 2.
Says my old one to your old one,
"Will you come to the Galway Races?"
Says your old one to my old one,
"With the price of my aul' lad's braces,
I went down to Capel Street
To see the money lenders,
But they wouldn't give me a couple of bob
On my aul' lad's suspenders."
CHORUS

Verse 3.
Says my old one to your old one,
"We have no beef or mutton,
But if we go to Monto town,
We might get a drink for nuttin'.
Here's a piece of advice
I got from an aul' fishmonger:
When food is scarce and you see a hearse,
You'll know you have died of hunger."
CHORUS

Does this melody sound familiar? It's the same as "The Girl I Left Behind Me." The lyrics reflect the dialogue between two housewives discussing their attempts to raise money so they could attend the annual picnic named for Dublin cobblers, called "waxies." The term "waxie" evolved from the shoemakers use of waxed thread on shoes for strength and water-proofing. The River Dargle was the site of the picnic, and the name "Dargle" became synonymous for all such outings.

THE WEARING OF THE GREEN

Ukulele tuning: gCEA

Traditional

Verse 1. Oh, Pad - dy dear and did you hear the news that's go - ing round? The

sham - rock is for - bid by law to grow on I - rish ground. No

more St. Pat - rick's Day we'll keep, his col - ors can't be seen, for

there's a cru - el law a - gainst the wear - ing of the green.

WHEN IRISH EYES ARE SMILING

Ukulele tuning: gCEA

**CHAUNCEY OLCOTT
and GEORGE GRAFF, JR.**

ERNEST R. BALL

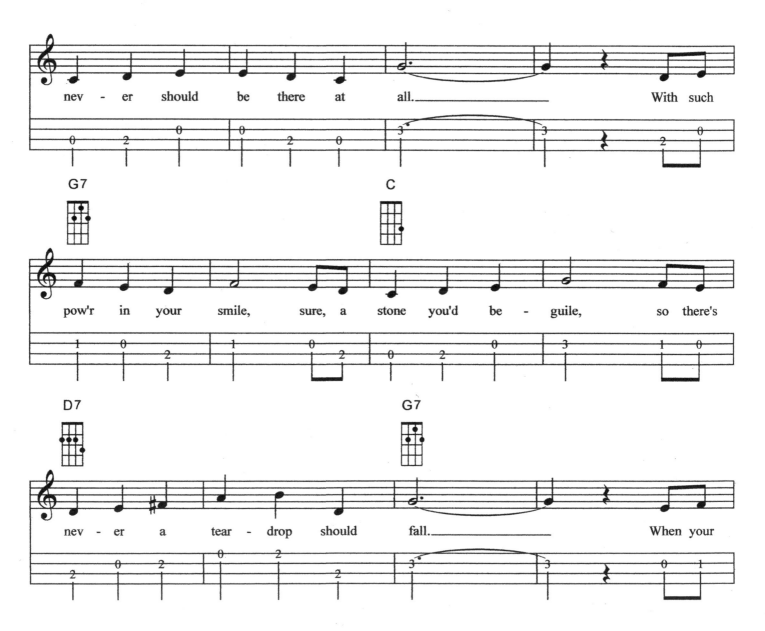

Verse 1. There's a tear in your eye, and I'm won-der-ing why, for it nev-er should be there at all._____ With such pow'r in your smile, sure, a stone you'd be - guile, so there's nev-er a tear-drop should fall._____ When your

WHEN IRISH EYES ARE SMILING

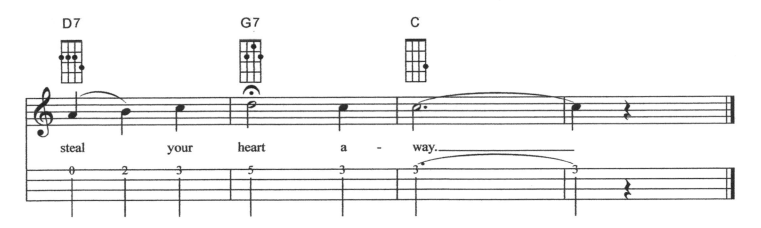

steal   your   heart   a - way.

Verse 2. For your smile is a part of the love in your heart,
And it makes even sunshine more bright;
Like the linnet's sweet song, crooning all the day long,
Comes your laughter so tender and light.
For the springtime of life is the sweetest of all,
There is ne'er a real care or regret;
And while springtime is ours,
Throughout all of youth's hours,
Let us smile each chance that we get.
CHORUS

Surely it is not an exaggeration to say that "When Irish Eyes Are Smiling" is probably the most popular of all Irish-American songs. Its co-lyricist, Chancellor "Chauncey" Olcott, was the personification of the consummate Irishman despite having been born in Buffalo, New York. But his ancestry was Irish and he paid tribute to it with stage performances, Broadway musicals he produced, and songs and lyrics he wrote -- all with an Irish theme. His singular efforts and collaborations can be found not only in "When Irish Eyes Are Smiling, but also in "My Wild Irish Rose," and "Mother Machree," to name just a few. Ernest Ball, although not Irish himself, wrote the music to many of these songs and the scores of Olcott's shows, as well as "A Little Bit Of Heaven" and the memorable "Let The Rest Of The World Go by."

WHEN YOU AND I WERE YOUNG, MAGGIE

Ukulele tuning: gCEA

Strictly speaking, this is not really an Irish song, although the name "Maggie" certainly qualifies as being Irish. The words were written as a poem by a Canadian school master inspired by one of his pupils whom he later married. The poem was set to music and the song continues to enjoy popularity after over 100 years. Of its numerous recordings, one is by the celebrated Irish tenor John McCormack, and that lends further justification for its inclusion here.

Words by
GEORGE W. JOHNSON

Music by
JAMES A. BUTTERFIELD

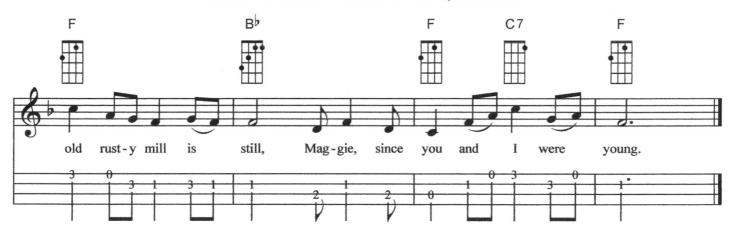

old rust-y mill is still, Mag-gie, since you and I were young.

Verse 2.
A city so silent and lone, Maggie,
(Where the young and the gay and the best
In polished white mansions of stone, Maggie,
Have each found a place of rest,)
Is built where the birds used to play, Maggie,
And join in the songs that were sung,
For we sang just as gay as they, Maggie,
When you and I were young.

Verse 3.
They say I am feeble with age, Maggie,
My steps are less sprightly than then,
My face is a well written page, Maggie,
But time alone was the pen.
They say we are aged and grey, Maggie,
As spray by the white breakers flung,
But to me you're as fair as you were, Maggie,
When you and I were young.

Verse 4. (Last eight measures)
And now we are aged and grey, Maggie,
The trials of life nearly done;
Let us sing of the days that are gone, Maggie,
When you and I were young.

WHERE THE RIVER SHANNON FLOWS

Ukulele tuning: gCEA

JAMES J. RUSSELL

Verse 1. There's a pret-ty spot in Ire-land I al-ways claim for my land, where the
Verse 2. Sure, no let-ter I'll be mail-ing, for soon I will be sail-ing, and I'll

fair - ies and the blar - ney will nev - er nev - er die. It's the
bless the ship that takes me to my dear old Er - in's shore. There I'll

land of the shil-le - lagh, my heart goes back there dai - ly, to the
set - tle down for-ev - er, I'll leave the old sod nev - er, and I'll

girl I left be - hind me when we kissed and said good - bye. Where
whis - per to my sweet-heart, "Come and take my name As - thore." Where

WHERE THE RIVER SHANNON FLOWS

WHISKEY IN THE JAR

Ukulele tuning: gCEA

Traditional

WHISKEY IN THE JAR

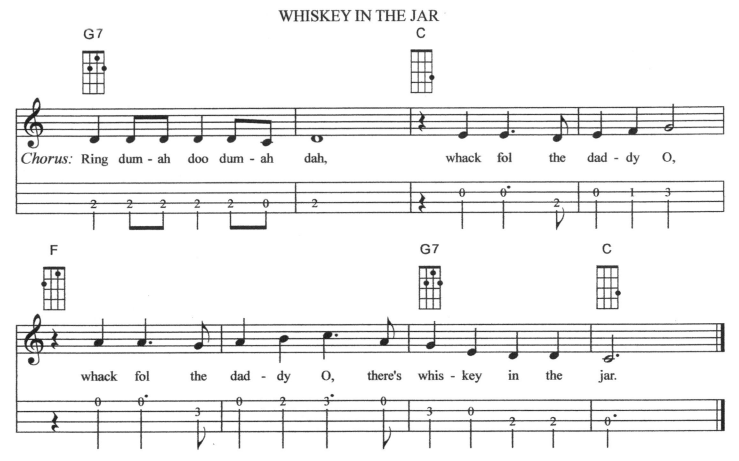

Chorus: Ring dum-ah doo dum-ah dah, whack fol the dad-dy O, whack fol the dad-dy O, there's whis-key in the jar.

Verse 2.

I counted out my money and it made a pretty penny,
I put it in my pocket and I gave it to my Jenny.
She sighed and she swore that she never would betray me,
But the devil take the women for they never can be easy.
CHORUS

Verse 3.

I went into my chamber for to take a slumber,
I dreamt of gold and jewels, and sure it was no wonder;
But Jenny took my charges and she filled them up with water,
Then she sent for Captain Farrell to be ready for the slaughter.
CHORUS

Verse 4.

'Twas early in the morning before I rose to travel,
The guards were all around me and likewise Colonel Farrell.
I then produced my pistol for she stole away my rapier,
But I couldn't shoot the water so a prisoner I was taken.
CHORUS

Verse 5.

And if anyone can help me it's my brother in the army,
I think that he is stationed in Cork or in Killarney.
And if he'd come and join me we'd go roving in Kilkenny;
I know he'd treat me fairer than my darling sporting Jenny.
CHORUS

THE WILD ROVER

Ukulele tuning: gCEA

Traditional

Verse 1. I've been a wild rov - er for man - y's the year, and I
spent all me mon - ey on whis - key and beer. And
now I'm re - turn - ing with gold in great store, and I
nev - er will play the wild rov - er no more. And it's

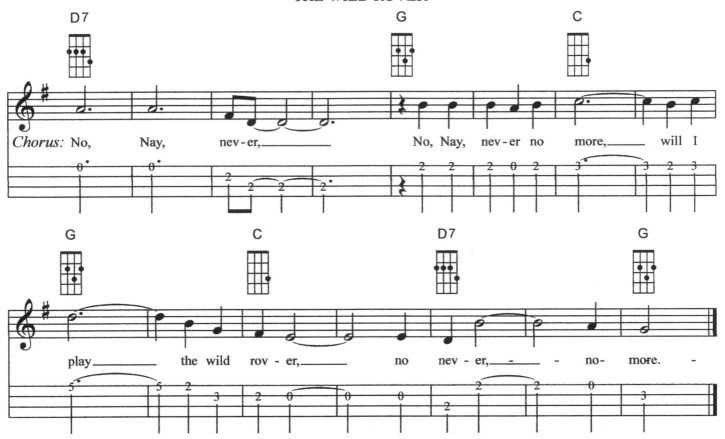

Verse 2.
I went to an alehouse I used to frequent,
And I told the landlady my money was spent.
I asked her for credit, she answered me, "Nay!
Such custom as yours I have every day."
CHORUS

Verse 3.
I took from my pocket ten sovereigns bright,
And the landlady's eyes opened wide with delight.
She said, "I have whiskey and wines of the best,
And the words that I told you were only in jest."
CHORUS

Verse 4.
I'll go home to my parents, confess what I've done,
And I'll ask them to pardon their prodigal son.
And when they've caressed me as oft times before,
I never will play the wild rover no more.
CHORUS

More Great Ukulele Books from Centerstream...